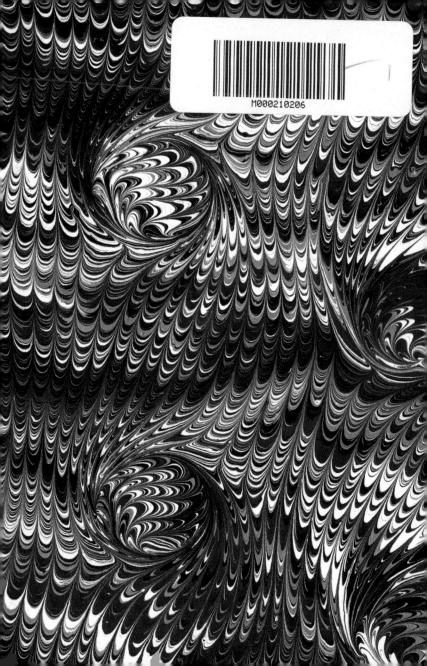

M000210206

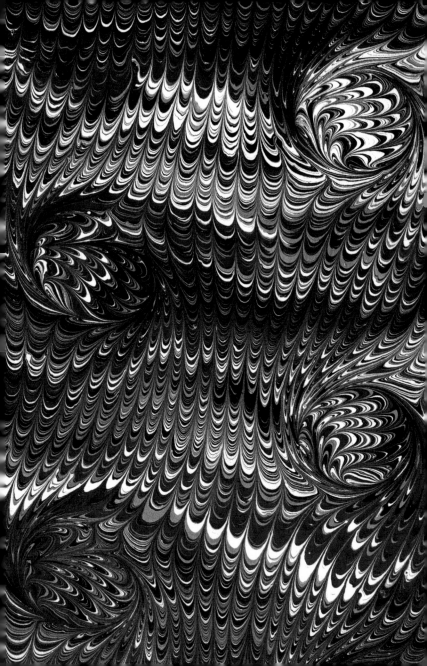

St Patrick's Breastplate

First published in 2006
by
Appletree Press Ltd
The Old Potato Station
14 Howard Street South
Belfast BT7 1AP

Tel: +44 (0) 28 90 24 30 74
Fax: +44 (0) 28 90 24 67 56
E-mail: reception@appletree.ie
Web Site: www.appletree.ie

Desk & Marketing Editor: Jean Brown
Copy-editing: Jim Black
Designer: Stuart Wilkinson
Production Manager: Paul McAvoy

St Patrick's Breastplate

ISBN-13: 978 0 86281 997 2
ISBN-10: 0 86281 997 0

St Patrick's
Breastplate

Introduction by Alf McCreary

Appletree Press

≈ INTRODUCTION ≈

'St. Patrick's Breastplate' is one of the most beautiful and best-loved hymns in the repertoire, and it was thought traditionally to have had its origins in a prayer by Ireland's Patron Saint himself.

Patrick, who grew up in Roman Britain in the 5th century AD, was the son of a deacon called Calpornius, and the grandson of Potitus, a priest or presbyter. At the age of 16 he was captured by a raiding party off a still-unidentified section of the coast of Roman Britain and taken as a slave to Ireland where he spent six years working as a shepherd at Slemish, in the north. It was here according to his autobiographical *Confessio* that he became a Christian. He wrote "…but after I came to Ireland – every day I had to tend sheep, and many times a day I prayed – the love of God and His fear came to me more and more, and my faith was strengthened."

He made a dramatic escape by boat from Ireland and after various adventures in Europe, possibly in Gaul, he went back to his parents. However in a dream he heard and saw a figure calling on him to return to Ireland. He did so, and as an ordained deacon, priest and Bishop he went back, between 425 and 435 AD. He died around 460 AD, possibly on 17 March, which is celebrated throughout the world as St. Patrick's Day. This tradition goes back to at least the 7th century.

According to legend, St. Patrick, who lived in difficult and dangerous times in 5th-century Ireland, wrote the prayer – which became popularly known later on as the hymn 'St. Patrick's Breastplate' – while he was travelling to Tara in Co. Meath as part of his missionary outreach. In making his way to Tara he was entering the territory of a hostile chieftain, one Loegaire MacNeill, who was said to be a supporter of the Druid fire-worshippers.

The chieftain laid an ambush for Patrick and his missionary colleagues, but as they proceeded they sang a version of the Saint's prayer, and they were mistaken for a herd of deer and allowed to pass by in safety. Hence a well-known alternative title for the prayer is 'The Deer's Cry', in the Gaelic 'Feath fiada'.

However, the prayer is also well-known as 'The Lorica' because of its association with the *lorica* – thought to be a spiritual form of breastplate armour. The significance went deeper in that the lorica was also thought to provide spiritual protection to those who wore it continually. It warded off not only illness and physical dangers, but it also promised a safe passage to heaven.

The connection between the 'Lorica' and the Christian writings of the New Testament is obvious. The Apostle Paul, for example, refers graphically in Ephesians to putting on "the whole armour of God that ye may be able to stand against the wiles of the devil". He also refers in Ephesians to "having on the breastplate of righteousness" and in First Thessalonians of "putting on the breastplate of faith and love."

The early Christians in Ireland would have understood easily this direct link between the 'Lorica' prayer and New Testament teaching. There would have been, however, an added significance for Patrick's time, in that the work had undertones which would have found a resonance in the Celtic Ireland of his Christian mission.

The idea of human beings being turned into a herd of deer by God for their own protection would have appealed to the vivid imagination of the Celts who believed that their ancient gods were eminently capable of changing their form. St. Patrick was a deeply spiritual and holy man, but he was also astute in worldly terms, and he knew how to co-exist with a Celtic people while carrying out his work of winning souls for God's kingdom. As he wrote in his celebrated 5th-century *Confessio* "it was most necessary to spread our nets so that a great multitude and throng might be caught for God, and that there be clerics everywhere to baptise, and exhort a people in need and want."

Though it is believed traditionally that Patrick wrote the Lorica prayer in Gaelic, and the last stanza in Latin (he was very proud of his Roman citizenship), scholars are divided on whether or not he was the author. Some feel that part of the language is Patrician, while others argue that while Patrician in sentiment, it differs from his known writing style and that it was composed by someone else – or by others – long after his death.

There is no doubt, however, that the claim on God's protection is essentially Patrician. In a memorable passage from his

Confessio, he outlines not only the considerable dangers facing a Christian missionary in 5th-century Ireland, but also the power of God in providing refuge and strength. Patrick, though he claimed to be uneducated, knew his Bible intimately, and this is clearly illustrated in his comments. He writes; "Daily I expect murder, fraud, or captivity or whatever it may be; but I fear none of these things because of the promises of heaven. I have cast myself into the hands of God Almighty, who rules everywhere, as the prophet says: 'Cast thy thought upon God and He shall sustain thee'."

'St. Patrick's Breastplate' has three distinct sections. It begins with the Invocation to the Holy Trinity, then a description of the various physical and bodily elements to be infused with God's protection, and also a list of those evils against which one needs to be protected – including "the demon snares of sin, the vice that gives temptation force, the natural lusts that war within, the hostile men that mar my course." However, the hymn ends triumphantly with the assertion "I bind unto myself the Name, the strong Name of the Trinity, by invocation of the same, the Three in One and One in Three."

The hymn-writer – Mrs Alexander

Various translations of the prayer were made, but by far the most popular setting today is that of the Irish hymn-writer Mrs Cecil Frances Alexander. It was commissioned at the end of the 19th century by H.H. Dickinson, Dean of the Chapel Royal in Dublin Castle, who wanted a metrical version of the work. He later wrote "I sent her a carefully-collated copy of the best prose versions, and within a week she sent me that exquisitely beautiful as well as faithful version which appears in the *Appendix* to our *Church Hymnal*." It was first used on 17 March, 1889.

Though the hymn is not easy to sing at the first attempt, the most popular musical setting is that of the Irish composer Sir Charles Villiers Stanford, while Mrs Alexander's metrical version is regarded as a masterpiece. She was so highly-regarded as a hymn-writer it is said that Charles Gounod, the distinguished French composer, once remarked "Some of her lyrics seemed to set themselves to music."

Known to her friends as "Fanny Alexander" she was born Cecil Frances Humphreys in Dublin in 1818, the third child of Elizabeth Reed and Major John Humphreys, originally from Norfolk. In 1850 she married a Church of Ireland clergyman, the Reverend William Alexander, who became Bishop of Derry and Raphoe in 1867. They had four children. Mrs Alexander died in Londonderry on 12 October, 1895. It is said that she was greatly beloved by the poor she had helped, and that thousands of people lined the route of her funeral cortege on its way to Derry Cemetery. Sadly, she died shortly before her husband became Archbishop of Armagh and Primate of All-Ireland, and served from 1896-1911.

Mrs Alexander had a strong social conscience, and she was actively involved in starting children's Sunday Schools and in improving the lot of women. The proceeds from the publication of her hymns were donated to help the deaf.

Throughout her lifetime, Mrs Alexander wrote more than 400 hymns, some of which remain widely popular to this day. They include the Christmas carol 'Once In Royal David's City' and 'There Is A Green Hill Far Away'. The music for the latter was written by William Horsley, a friend of Mendelssohn.

Mrs Alexander had a gift for communicating with children, and her children's hymn 'All Things Bright And Beautiful' has been sung and recorded in many different versions, ranging from a church setting to various interpretations by popular musicians of the day. There is no doubt, however, that one of her crowning achievements was her metrical version of 'St. Patrick's Breastplate'.

- Alf McCreary, MBE

St Patrick's
Breastplate

bind
unto
myself
today

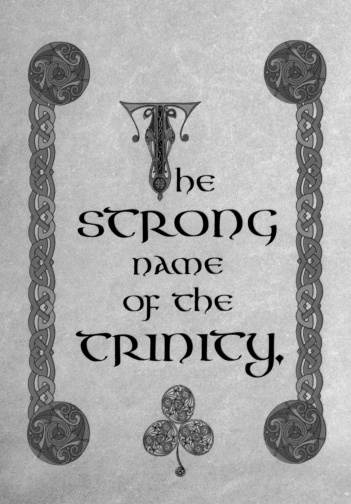

The
STRONG
name
of the
TRINITY.

By
invocation
of the
SAME,

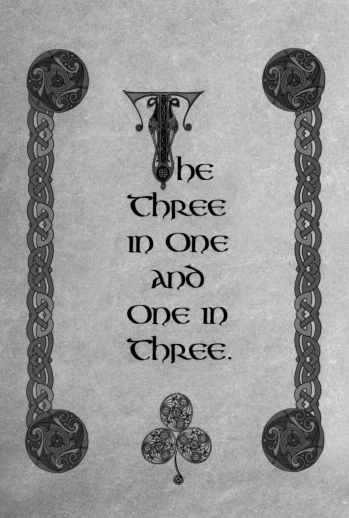

The
Three
in One
and
One in
Three.

I bind
this day
to me
for ever.

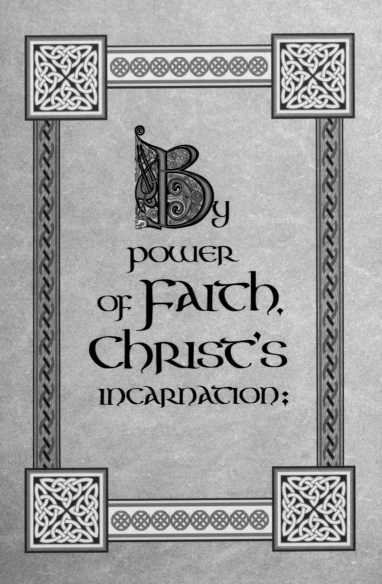

By
power
of FAITH,
CHRIST'S
INCARNATION;

His Baptism in the Jordan river;

His
death on
Cross
for my
salvation;

his
bursting
from the
spicèd
tomb;

His
riding up
the
heavenly
way;

His
coming at
the day
of doom;

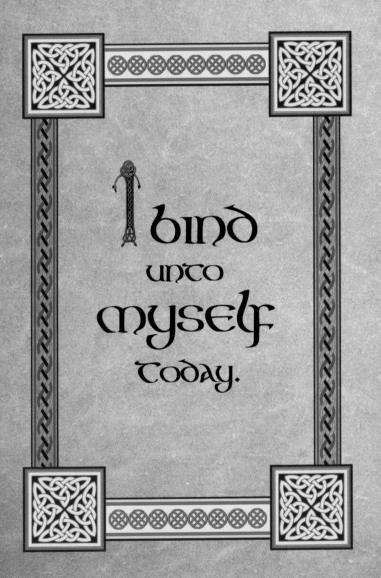

I bind
unto
myself
today.

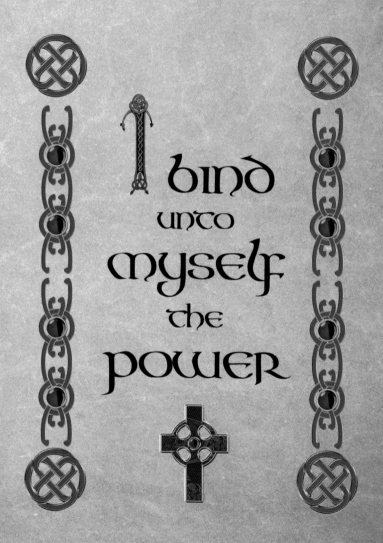

I bind
unto
myself
the
POWER

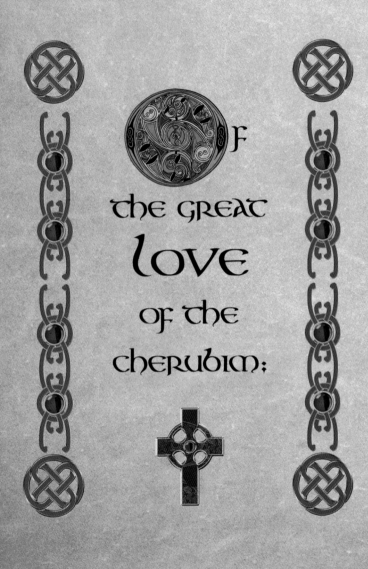

Of the great love of the cherubim;

The
sweet
'well done'
in
judgement
hour;

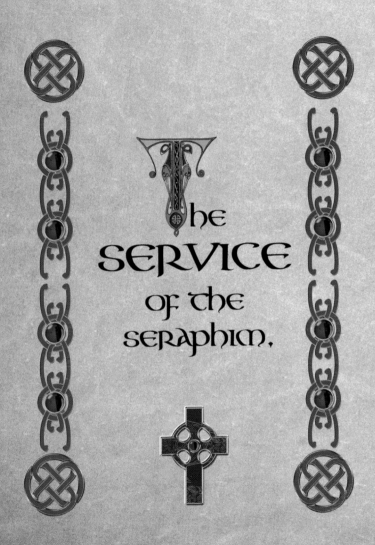

The SERVICE OF THE SERAPHIM.

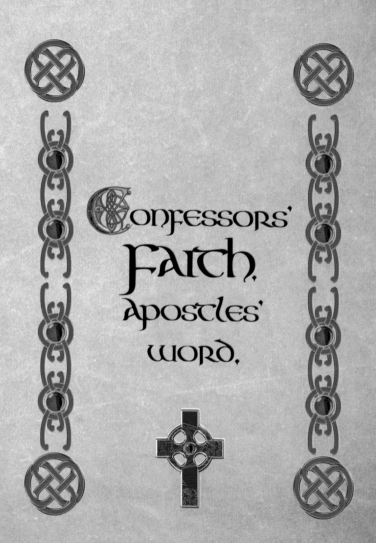

Confessors' Faith, Apostles' Word,

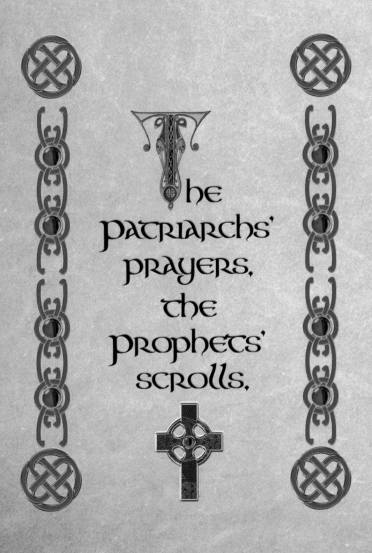

The
Patriarchs'
Prayers,
the
Prophets'
Scrolls.

All good
deeds
done unto
the
LORD.

And
purity
of
virgin
souls.

I
bind
unto
myself
today

The
VIRTUES
OF THE
STARLIT
HEAVEN.

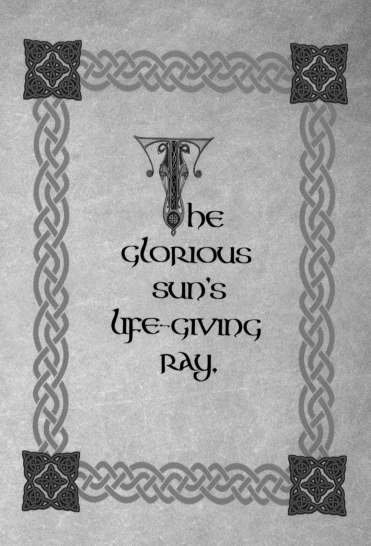

The
Glorious
sun's
life-giving
ray.

The whiteness of the moon at even,

The
Flashing
of the
lightning
free,

The
whirling
wind's
tempestuous
shocks,

The
stable earth,
the
deep salt
sea,

Around
the old
ETERNAL
rocks.

I

bind

unto

myself

today

The
POWER
of
GOD
to hold
and lead.

His
eye to
watch,
his
might to
stay,

His
ear to
hearken
to my
need.

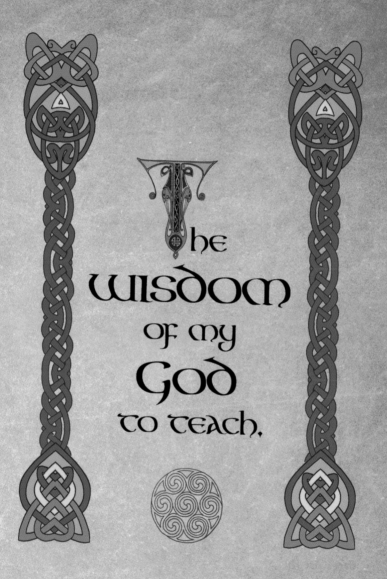

The
wisdom
of my
God
to teach,

44

His
hand to
guide,
his
shield to
ward.

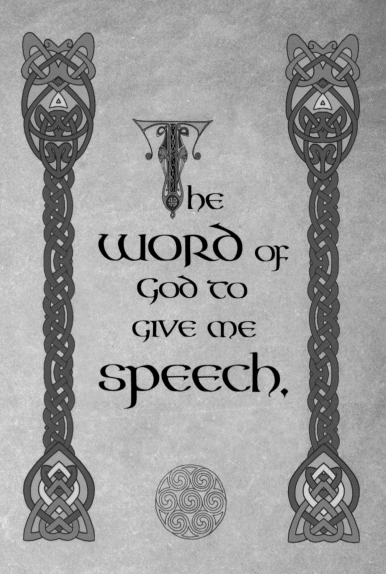

The WORD OF GOD TO GIVE ME speech.

His
heavenly
host
to be my
GUARD.

Against
the
Demon
snares of
SIN,

The
VICE
that gives
temptation
force,

The

natural lusts

that WAR

within.

The
hostile men
that MAR
my course:

Or
Few or
many,
far or
nigh.

In
EVERY
place
and in all
hours

Against their FIERCE hostility.

 bind
to me
these holy
POWERS.

AGAINST all SATAN'S spells and wiles,

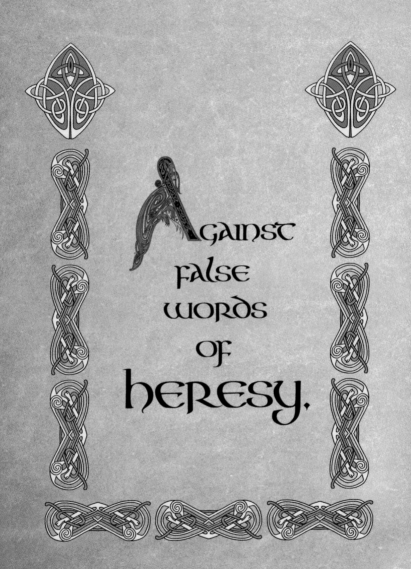

Against false words of heresy.

57

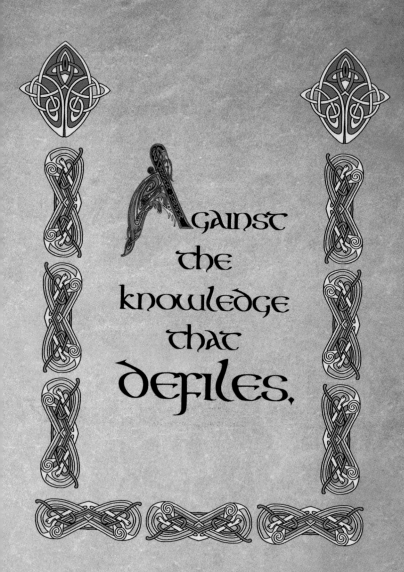

Against
the
knowledge
that
Defiles,

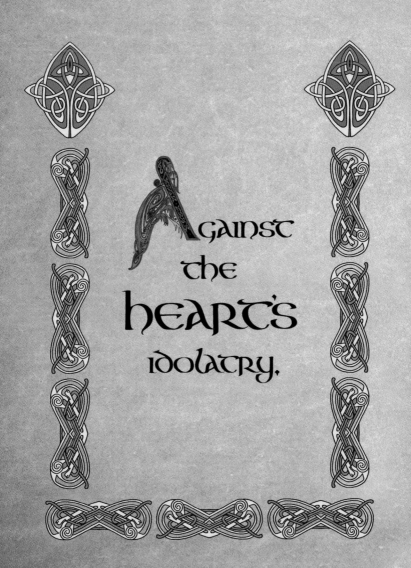

Against the Heart's idolatry,

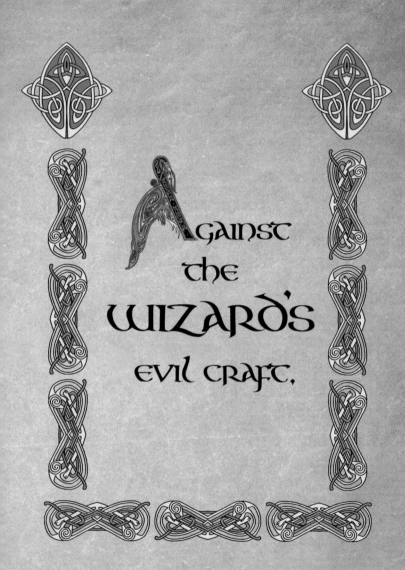

Against the WIZARD'S evil craft,

Against the death wound and the burning

The choking
WAVE
and the
poisoned
shaft.

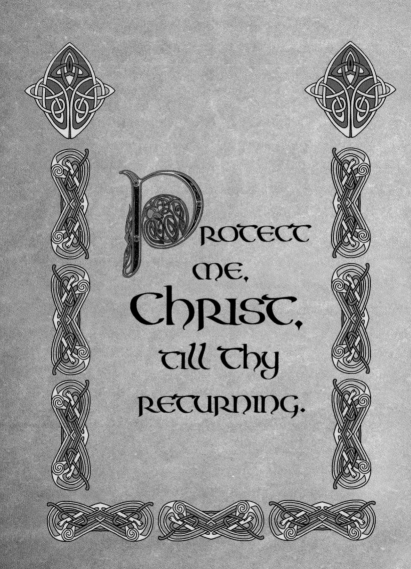

PROTECT ME, CHRIST, TILL THY RETURNING.

Christ
be with me,
Christ
within me,

Christ
behind me,
Christ
before me,

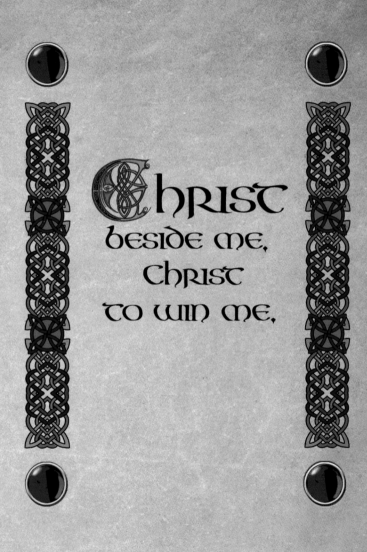

Christ
beside me,
Christ
to win me,

Christ
to
comfort
and
restore
me,

CHRIST
beneath me,
CHRIST
above me,

Christ
in quiet,
Christ
in danger,

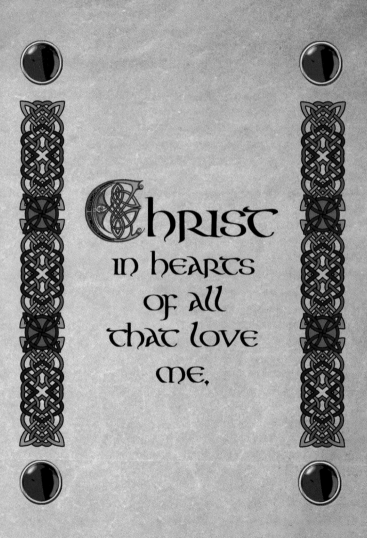

CHRIST
in hearts
of all
that love
me,

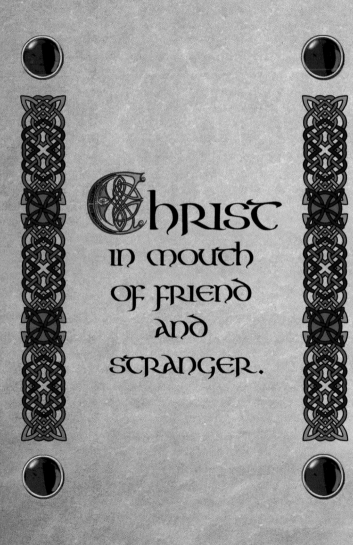

Christ
in mouth
of friend
and
stranger.

I
bind
unto
myself
the name,

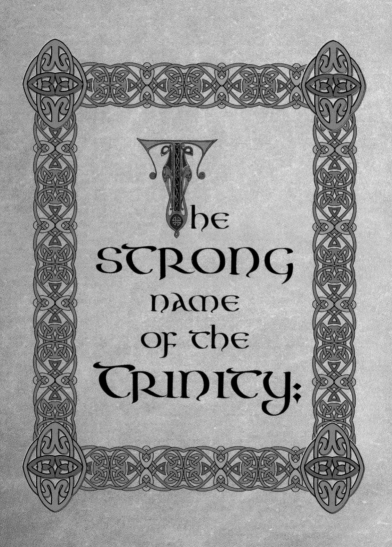

The
STRONG
name
of the
TRINITY;

By
invocation
of the
SAME.

The
Three
in One,
and
One in
Three,

Of
whom all
NATURE
hath
CREATION,

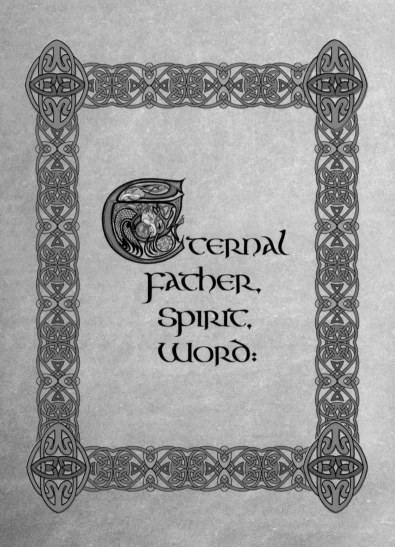

ETERNAL
FATHER,
SPIRIT,
WORD:

Praise to
the
Lord
of my
salvation.

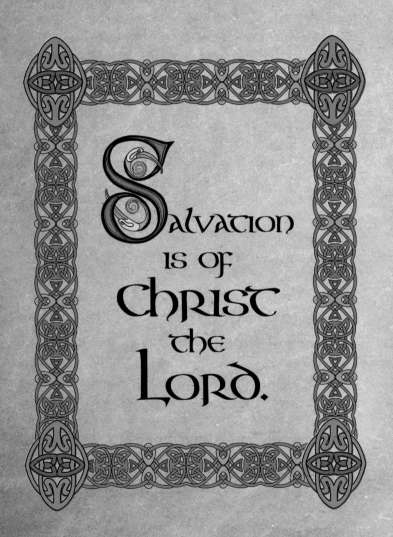

Salvation is of Christ the Lord.

Bibliography

Commemoration Notes on Cecil Frances Alexander, St. Anne's Cathedral, Belfast 2005.

Companion to Church Hymnal edited by Bishop Edward Darling and Dr Donald Davison, published by The Columba Press, Dublin 2005.

A Green Hill Far Away: The Life of Mrs CF Alexander by W.O. Ernest, published in Dublin and London by SPCK and APCK, 1970.

St. Patrick's City – The Story of Armagh by Alf McCreary, The Blackstaff Press, Belfast 2001.

Mrs Alexander: A life of the Hymn-writer Cecil Frances Alexander 1818-1895 by Valerie Wallace, published by The Lilliput Press 1995.

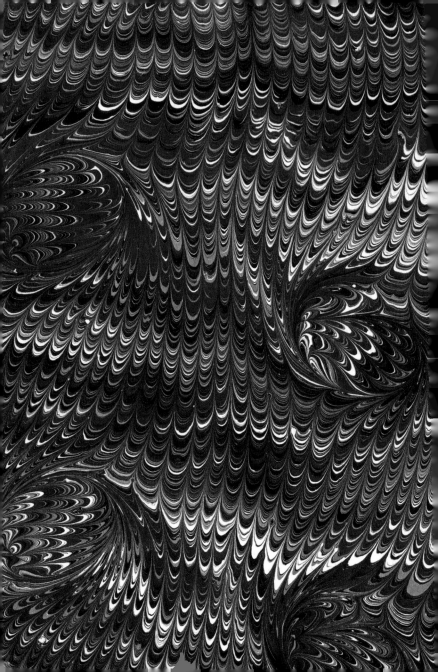